Searchlight
BOOKS™

How Do
We Use
Money?

Earning Income

Bitsy Kemper

Lerner Publications
Minneapolis

Lerner Publications Company
A division of Lerner Publishing Group, Inc.
241 First Avenue North
Minneapolis, MN 55401 USA

For reading levels and more information, look up this title at www.lernerbooks.com.

Content consultant: Donna Little, Associate Professor of Accounting and Finance, Menlo College

Library of Congress Cataloging-in-Publication Data

Kemper, Bitsy.
        Earning income / by Bitsy Kemper.
            pages   cm. — (Searchlight books—how do we use money?)
        Includes index.
        ISBN 978-1-4677-5227-5 (lib. bdg. : alk. paper)
        ISBN 978-1-4677-6253-3 (EB pdf)
        1. Wages—Juvenile literature. 2. Income—Juvenile literature. 3. Money—
    Juvenile literature. I. Title.
        HD4909.K44 2015
        339.2'2—dc23   2014019888

Manufactured in the United States of America
1 — BP — 12/31/14

Contents

Chapter 1

PAID TO WORK

You can earn money in many ways. Working at a job is one way. The money you earn from a job is called income. Many different jobs are available. Each job needs different skills. Adults can choose jobs based on their skills.

Helping out at a garage sale is one way kids can earn money. What is the money you earn from a job called?

Accountants have strong math skills. Artists see things in exciting new ways. Doctors are experts in the human body. Kids can find jobs that fit their skills too. Are you good with numbers? Maybe you could handle money at a garage sale. Are you creative? You could make bracelets to sell. Do you love animals? Try dog walking.

WALKING DOGS NOT ONLY GIVES YOU EXTRA SPENDING MONEY BUT ALSO FRESH AIR AND EXERCISE.

Nursing is a career. Working as a nurse requires specialized training and education.

Job or Career?

People use the terms *job* and *career* to describe their work. But jobs are different from careers. A job is any task that someone does to earn money. Working as a cashier over the summer is a job. So is taking tickets at a movie theater. A career is a job that someone usually does for a long time after having special training. Teaching is a career. Nursing is also a career.

People usually do not begin a career until they are adults. But you do not need to wait until then to think about careers. It is never too early to figure out what your skills and interests are.

Getting Paid

Income is paid in a few different ways. People who earn hourly wages get paid for each hour they work. This is a common way to get paid in stores. The more hours these people work, the more money they make.

Workers who earn hourly wages sometimes use machines that count their hours. They slide a card into the machine when they arrive and again when they leave. Both times are marked on the card.

Most office workers get paid
salaries rather than hourly wages.

Some people earn salaries. This means they earn a certain amount each year. They get part of that amount in each paycheck. For example, a worker might get paid every two weeks. Each paycheck would have one twenty-sixth of her salary. People who work in offices often get paid this way. They work for a certain number of hours. Many salaried people work forty hours per week. Often they work five eight-hour days each week. They do not make extra money for working more hours.

Other people earn money on commission. This means they earn money based on the amount of work they do. Salespeople usually work on commission. They earn a portion of the sales they make. They are paid only when a sale is completed. Real estate agents are often paid on commission. They earn part of the sale price when they sell a house.

 # Decision Time

A neighbor will pay you to rake leaves in his yard. It will take you one hour to rake the yard. Then it will take ten more minutes to bag each pile and bring it to the curb. He will either pay you $4 per bag of leaves or $10 per hour. You get to decide. You have raked for him before. You know you usually fill six bags with leaves. Would you choose the per-bag rate or the hourly wage?

Trade school students learn practical skills, such as auto and motorcycle repair.

Greater Skills and Greater Pay

Your first job does not have to be your only job. You can learn new skills to open up new job options. Going to college is one way to open up more options. Employers are often willing to pay more for educated workers. Trade school is another way to find a higher-paying job. These schools teach people specific skills. Students can learn things such as auto repair and plumbing. These skills make them valuable to employers.

Experience can also help start a new career. You can get experience by volunteering. If you want to work with animals, you could volunteer at an animal shelter. If you already have a job, you could ask your boss for new or different job responsibilities. This can give you more experience in your current job.

College and trade school can increase your income. However, they also cost time and money. Gaining new experience takes time too. It may take hard work, but you can find jobs that pay well and make you happy.

Did You Know?

Scientists have studied whether money makes people happy. In 2011, a student at Illinois Wesleyan University looked at several of these studies. He found something interesting. His research showed that more money did not make people happy. Instead, happier people made more money! The research suggested people with a positive attitude earn more than other workers.

Chapter 2

MAKING A PROFIT

If you run a business, one way to earn money is by making a profit. It costs money to run a business. This money makes up the expenses. The money a business takes in is called revenue. After revenue covers all the expenses, the extra money is profit. When a company sells shoes for $50, that $50 is revenue.

Companies that sell products, such as shoes, earn money when they sell a product. What is this money called?

If the shoes cost the company $40 to make, the company earns $10 in profit.

Costs and Prices

People who start businesses are called entrepreneurs. They take risks. Their business ideas always have the chance to fail. If a business fails, an entrepreneur could lose money. However, a business may become very popular. The payoff from starting a successful business can be huge.

Being an entrepreneur takes a lot of research and hard work.

Running a business is not just for adults. Kids can run some businesses themselves. One example is a lemonade stand.

Imagine you run a lemonade stand of your own. You sell each cup of lemonade for 50¢. At the end of the day, you sell twenty cups, adding up to $10 in revenue. Did you make enough money to cover your costs and earn a profit? It depends on your costs.

You need to keep track of how much it costs to make the lemonade. This includes the costs of cups, sugar, lemons, and other supplies. You also need to think about what it cost to set up the stand. All these costs can add up quickly.

Lemonade stands are common businesses run by kids.

Lemonade 50¢

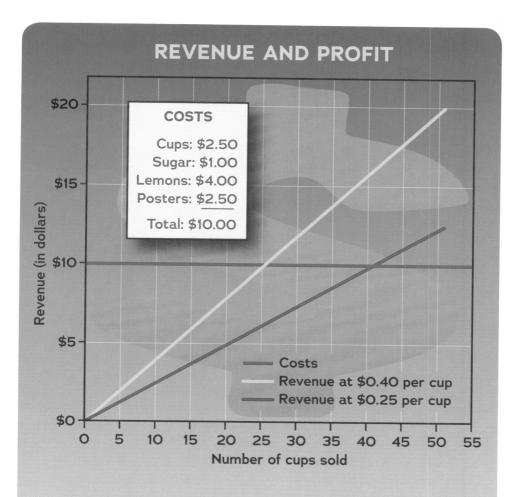

REVENUE AND PROFIT

COSTS

Cups: $2.50
Sugar: $1.00
Lemons: $4.00
Posters: $2.50

Total: $10.00

Revenue (in dollars)

Number of cups sold

— Costs
— Revenue at $0.40 per cup
— Revenue at $0.25 per cup

Turning revenue into profit depends on many factors. They include costs, prices, and the number of sales. Take a look at this graph for a lemonade stand's sales. It shows how revenue grows over time. Revenue grows faster if you sell lemonade at 40¢ rather than 25¢. Adding a line for costs can show how soon you will make a profit. As soon as the revenue line goes over the costs line, the lemonade stand is making a profit.

Sometimes businesses will give discounts or free products to their employees.

If it costs you 55¢ to make a cup of lemonade you sell for 50¢, you made no profit. You lost 5¢ for each cup you sold. To make a profit, you need to raise the selling price. Prices are based on what people are willing to spend. Imagine people are willing to spend 75¢ on a cup of lemonade. If you charge 50¢, you are giving up 25¢ per sale. If no one will pay 50¢, you will have to lower your prices. You may stop making a profit at the lower price. You might have to find ways to lower your costs.

Selling

Another way kids can make money is by selling things they own. Garage sales and online auction sites let you sell used goods. You may sell old toys or clothes. It costs money to sell things, but the cost is usually small. You must spend time organizing the items. You may have to make signs for a garage sale. Selling online means you will have to pay for shipping costs.

 Did You Know?

Jaden, aged twelve, and his sister Amaya, aged eleven, live in Tennessee. They run their own business. It started when their mom challenged them to make their own money. They decided to sell snow cones. The kids started by selling the treats from a table in their front yard. In two years, they had made enough money to buy their own food truck. However, their mom drives them around. It will still be a few years before they can drive themselves!

However, you should ask a parent before selling things. This is especially important if a parent bought the item. He or she might want to put the money back into the family budget. Or your parent might not want to sell the item at all.

Another way to make money is to sell things you have made. You could make bracelets or carve wooden sculptures. You can also sell services, such as petsitting or garden weeding. These are some of the most popular ways for kids to earn extra money.

Garage sales give you a chance to clean out your home and make some money.

Decision Time

You won a brand-new laptop in a raffle. The ticket cost $1. But you already have a computer that works just fine. How can you turn the winning prize into profit? Which of these three options would you choose?

1. Keep the new computer. Sell the one you already have for $150. The raffle ticket cost $1, so you would make a $149 profit. You could spend that profit on games for your new computer. You could also save it in the bank or donate some to charity.

2. Sell the brand-new computer for $300. Keep using the one you already have. You could use the $299 profit to upgrade your current computer. You might even have enough left to save some in the bank and give some to charity.

3. Keep and use both computers. You would not get a profit, but you might prefer to have an extra computer around.

Chapter 3

OTHER INCOME SOURCES

In addition to working or running a business, you can earn income in a few other ways. One is to simply keep your money in a bank. When you put money into a savings account, you earn interest. Interest is money that the bank pays you to keep your money there.

Keeping your money in a bank is another way to earn income. What is the money you earn called?

Interest is calculated as a percentage of the money in your account. For example, if you earn 2 percent interest on $100, you will earn $2. Interest is often very small. The percentage may change over time. Interest is not a fast way to earn income. But it is a good way to earn extra cash while keeping your money safe.

You can also earn money from investments. One way to invest is to buy stock. Stock is a small piece of a company. When the company does well, your stock is worth more. Then you can sell it for more money than you paid for it. It may take a long time to make a profit, however. People may hold onto stocks for years before selling them. But there is also a risk the company will do poorly. If that happens, the value of the stock may go down. Investors lose money when stocks drop.

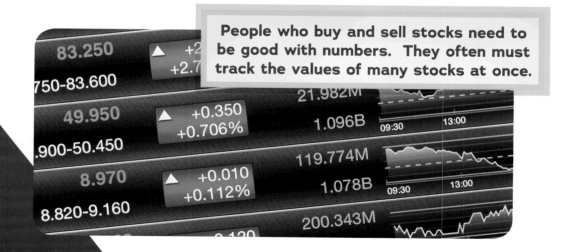

People who buy and sell stocks need to be good with numbers. They often must track the values of many stocks at once.

It can be tempting to spend birthday money all at once, but it may be better to save it. Waiting awhile before buying something gives you time to think about your purchases.

One common source of income for kids is gifts. You might get cash on your birthday or on holidays. It can be exciting to get money as a gift. It helps you reach your savings goals faster. It may also let you buy expensive items. However, you should not treat gift money as a steady source of income. You never know for sure whether you will get it.

IF A PERSON IS GOOD AT MANAGING PROPERTIES, RENTING OUT A HOME CAN BE A STEADY SOURCE OF INCOME.

For Rent

Adults can earn income from renting out homes. This is known as rental income. It may seem like an easy way to make money. But renting is hard work. You must make sure your property stays clean. You have to fix things that break. And you need to find reliable renters to live in your property.

Kids may consider renting out things they already own. Kids rarely rent out property to make money. It could happen, though. Imagine you live near a popular beach. If you own a surfboard, you could rent it to tourists. If you

BIKE RENTALS ARE OFTEN POPULAR WITH TOURISTS IN SIGHTSEEING AREAS.

want to rent something, be sure to check with a parent first. An adult should be involved in case something goes wrong. An item could be lost or damaged. Kids usually do not rent things to their friends. Friends probably expect to borrow things for free.

Decision Time

You live near a beach where people vacation. You decide to rent out your bike to earn income. You need to spend $25 to repair and clean your bike so people will want to rent it. You estimate you can rent it ten times this summer for either $2, $3, $4, or $5. However, if you charge $6, you think you will be able to rent it only eight times. You are pretty sure no one will want to rent it for $7. You want to make sure you are earning a profit. How much should you charge to rent the bike?

Allowances give kids a chance to practice spending, saving, and budgeting.

Allowances

More than 60 percent of US kids earn an allowance. An allowance is money parents give to kids. Most kids start getting it by the age of eight. Allowances are another kind of income. Having some spending money helps kids learn how to spend and save wisely. Most US parents pay between 50¢ and $1 per week for each year of their child's age.

Allowances do not have to be based on chores. Most parents think kids should help out at home regardless of allowance. Some families offer other ways for kids to earn money. A kid could do extra chores, such as weeding a garden or giving the dog a bath. Earning an allowance helps kids practice dealing with money. Experience with money can help a kid grow into a money-smart adult.

Did You Know?

Only about 1 percent of kids save any of their allowances. However, saving even a small amount can add up to a lot over time. The average allowance in the United States is about $780 per year. If you saved that much for fifteen years and put it in an investment that earns 6 percent per year, you would have nearly $20,000!

Chapter 4

INCOME TAXES

People in the United States do not keep all the money they earn. Americans must pay part of their income to the government. This is called income tax. The federal government collects this tax. The group that handles these taxes is the Internal Revenue Service.

The US government collects and spends tax money. What is the name of the group within the government that handles income taxes?

Tax Dollars at Work

Who pays the electric bill on streetlights? Who pays for roads and schools? The government uses tax money to pay for goods and services. It pays for things that benefit the public. This includes goods such as traffic lights and parks. It also includes services such as police departments. Taxes also pay for the military and health care.

Taxes help pay for police and many other public services.

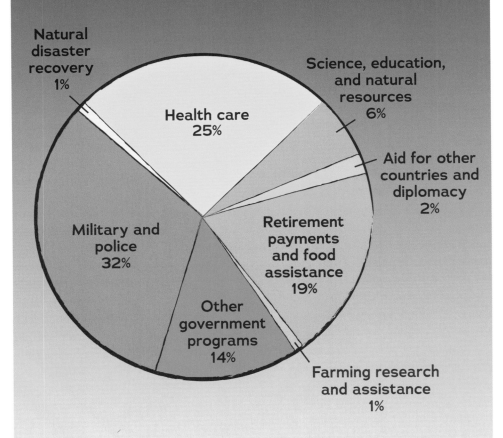

WHERE YOUR INCOME TAX DOLLAR GOES

Natural disaster recovery 1%

Health care 25%

Science, education, and natural resources 6%

Aid for other countries and diplomacy 2%

Military and police 32%

Retirement payments and food assistance 19%

Other government programs 14%

Farming research and assistance 1%

This graph shows where each dollar of income tax money goes. For example, the government spends 32 cents out of each dollar of income tax it collects on the military and police.

The income tax you pay depends on how much you earn. The government sets different percentages for different income levels. These are tax brackets. Each bracket covers certain percentages, or rates. In 2013, the rate was 10 percent for people making up to $8,925 per year. This was the lowest tax bracket. If you made between $8,926 and $36,250, you move into the next bracket. This higher bracket is taxed at 15 percent.

MANY PEOPLE FILL OUT A FORM CALLED A 1040 TO PAY THEIR TAXES.

▼

Form **1040** Department of the Treasury—Internal Revenue Service (99) 2

U.S. Individual Income Tax Return

For the year Jan. 1–Dec. 31

Your first name and initial | Last name

If a joint return, spouse's first name and initial | Last name

Home address (number and street). If you have a P.O. box, see instructions.

City, town or post office, state, and ZIP code. If you have a foreign address, also comple | Forei

Foreign country name

Filing Status

1 ☐ Single
2 ☐ Married filing jointly (even if only o
   ☐ d filing separately.

Some people's taxes get very complicated. They may hire an accountant to help them fill out their paperwork.

The percentages apply only to their own brackets. You pay 15 percent only on the income between $8,926 and $36,250. For example, imagine you made $9,025 in 2013. The first $8,925 is taxed at 10 percent. This comes to $892.50 in taxes. The last $100 of your income is taxed at 15 percent. This comes to $15. So your total tax is $907.50.

The highest bracket in 2013 was for people who made more than $400,000. They were taxed at 39.6 percent for any income over $400,000.

Work income is taxed differently than investment income. Usually, investment income is taxed less.

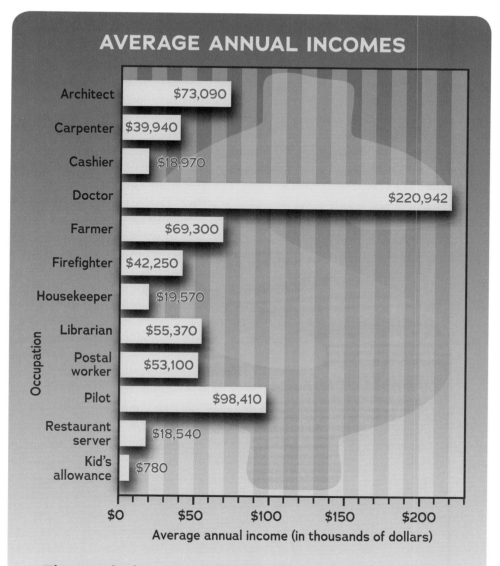

AVERAGE ANNUAL INCOMES

Occupation	Average annual income (in thousands of dollars)
Architect	$73,090
Carpenter	$39,940
Cashier	$18,970
Doctor	$220,942
Farmer	$69,300
Firefighter	$42,250
Housekeeper	$19,570
Librarian	$55,370
Postal worker	$53,100
Pilot	$98,410
Restaurant server	$18,540
Kid's allowance	$780

This graph shows average incomes in the United States for different jobs in 2012. The information comes from the Bureau of Labor Statistics, a government group that collects data about workers and careers.

Taxes and Kids

You might think only adults have to worry about taxes. But some kids pay income taxes too. Most kids do not earn enough money to have to pay income taxes.

Still, laws change often, so it is a good idea to look up the current rules. In 2013, you had to pay income taxes if you fit into one of two groups. First, you had to pay if you earned more than $1,000 from investments. Second, you had to pay if you earned more than $6,100 from work.

Kids can invest with a parent's help. If you do invest, check with a parent or a banker to see if you need to pay taxes.

Kids usually do not fit into either group. Still, if you earn any income, a parent can let you know if you will need to pay taxes. Many people dislike paying taxes. Taxes mean less money in your pocket. But remember that taxes pay for important things. Police keep our cities safe. Roads help us easily move from place to place.

Your income lets you pay for the things you need. People have many choices of how to earn income. They can choose jobs that fit their interests. They can grow their income by learning new skills. They can even start their own businesses. Knowing how you get money is the first step in making smart money decisions.

Learning how to make money helps teach you how to use money.

Top Ten Things to Know

1. You can earn income by working.

2. Many different careers are available.

3. You can earn money at a job through hourly wages, yearly salaries, or on commission.

4. You can increase your income and job opportunities by getting more education, more work experience, and the right job skills.

5. You can earn income through interest, rent, business profit, and investments.

6. Profit is revenue minus all the costs of doing business.

7. Prices are based on what people are willing to pay.

8. Part of people's income is collected by the government as income tax.

9. Taxes allow the government to pay for public goods and services.

10. Most kids do not have to pay income tax. You can check with a parent to find out if this includes you.

Glossary

allowance: money parents give to kids

career: a job that someone usually does for many years after having special training

commission: money made from the sale of a good or service

entrepreneur: a person who starts a business

interest: money a bank pays you to keep your money with them

job: work done to earn money

profit: revenue minus costs

revenue: the money made on the sale of goods or services

salary: a fixed amount of money earned in exchange for doing a job

stock: a small part of a company that anyone can purchase

Expand learning beyond the printed book. Download free, complementary educational resources for this book from our website, www.lerneresource.com.

Learn More about Money

Books

Bernstein, Daryl. *Better Than a Lemonade Stand!: Small Business Ideas for Kids.* New York: Aladdin, 2012. This book is filled with more than fifty ways that kids can earn money. The updated version includes new information on the Internet and social media.

Jacobsen, Ryan. *Get a Job Making Stuff to Sell.* Minneapolis: Lerner Publications, 2015. This book will walk you through the basics of making things to sell. It also offers tips and tricks on how to get started.

Orr, Tamra. *A Kid's Guide to Earning Money.* Hockessin, DE: Mitchell Lane, 2009. How do you know if a job is right for you? What jobs are you allowed to work? Follow along with fifth graders as they figure out how to earn enough money to go on a field trip.

Websites

How to Make Money as a Kid
http://money.howstuffworks.com/personal-finance/budgeting/make-money-kid.htm
Check out ten clever ways to earn some spending money, from crafting to inventions. This site offers beginning steps and suggested age ranges for each idea.

It's My Life: Making Money
http://pbskids.org/itsmylife/money/making
This website talks about the ways kids can earn income. It also features stories from real-life kids and talks about the ways they have earned money.

Oregon Museum of Science and Industry: Lemonade Stand
https://www.omsi.edu/exhibits/moneyville/activities/lemonade/lemonadestand.htm
This game gives you the chance to try running your own lemonade stand. Research the market, set prices, and decide how much lemonade to make. See if you can make a profit!

Index

Photo Acknowledgments

The images in this book are used with the permission of: © David Sacks/Digital Vision/Thinkstock, p. 4; © Mike Flippo/Shutterstock Images, p. 5; © spwidoff/Shutterstock Images, p. 6; © Alexey Stiop/Shutterstock Images, p. 7; © Monkey Business Images/Shutterstock Images, p. 8; © Goodluz/Shutterstock Images, p. 10; © Natali Glado/Shutterstock Images, p. 12; © auremar/Shutterstock Images, p. 13; © Rob Marmion/Shutterstock Images, p. 14; © Laura Westlund/Independent Picture Service, pp. 15, 30, 33; © Annika Erickson/Blend RM/Glow Images, p. 16; © trekandshoot/Thinkstock, p. 18; © Phototreat/Thinkstock, p. 20; © leungchopan/Shutterstock Images, p. 21; © Jeka/Shutterstock Images, p. 22; © Andy Dean Photography/Shutterstock Images, p. 23; © Denise Lett/Shutterstock Images, p. 24; © John Howard/Thinkstock, p. 26; © kropic1/Shutterstock Images, p. 28; © John Roman Images/Shutterstock Images, p. 29; © Bunwit Unseree/Shutterstock Images, p. 31; © Jupiterimages/Creatas Images/Thinkstock, p. 32; © JaysonPhotography/iStock/Thinkstock, p. 34; © Ryan McVay/Thinkstock, p. 35; © Catherine Yeulet/iStock/Thinkstock, p. 36; © Atlaspix/Shutterstock Images, pp. 9, 11, 17, 19, 25, 27; © Carolyn Franks/Shutterstock Images, p. 27.

Front cover: © Stockbyte/Thinkstock, (coins); © Laura Westlund/Independent Picture Service (illustration).

Main body text set in Adrianna Regular 14/20.
Typeface provided by Chank.